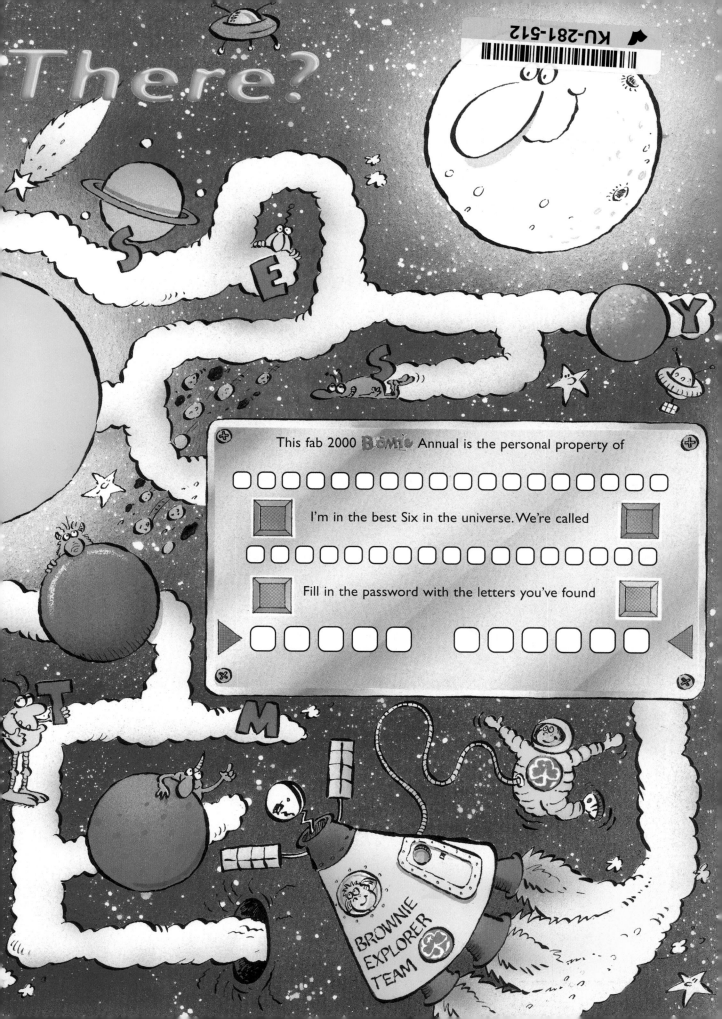

Brownie Guides

The fun-packed Brownie programme is bursting with exciting activities. Just one amazing reason to be a Brownie!

Go!

Go! is a special part of your Brownie programme for nine-year-olds. Don't let this stop you having a go at these pages though!

Brownie Guide Law

A Brownie Guide thinks of others before herself and does a Good Turn every day.

My Brownie Guide Promise

I promise that I will do my best:
To love my God,
To serve the Queen and my country,
To help other people and
To keep the Brownie Guide Law.

Brownie Guide Motto

Lend a hand.

If you see this sign, ask a grown-up you know for help. You can still do it all by yourself, but make sure an adult says OK and is watching what you do. If there isn't a sign and you're not sure about something, it's always best to ask an adult you know for help. It's good to be safe!

Badges

Some of the ideas and activities in this great Annual can help you with badges. Or you may fancy having a go at a badge after you've read one of the fantastic features. If you want to find out what you have to do to get the badge, look it up in your *Brownie Guide Badge Book*. For most badges there are a few things you need to do, but the most important thing is to always do your very best.

Brownies are friendly

Brownies are wide awake

Brownies have fun out-of-doors

Brownies help at home

Brownies keep healthy

Brownies lend a hand

Brownies make things

Brownies do their best

These badges show which part of your Brownie programme is being covered.

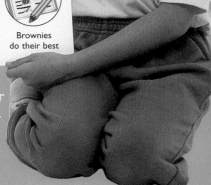

THE GUIDE ASSOCIATION
A registered charity

Brownie
Annual 2000

Find out what the special symbols in your fab 2000 Brownie Annual mean!

Leave a message for me at www.guides.org.uk

Freda
Freda helps you remember your Brownie Guide Promise. All through your Annual she's got loads of ideas and suggestions. Watch out for her!

Web safe
My Brownie code for safety on the World Wide Web. I promise that:
- I will agree with my parent(s)'/guardian(s)' rules for me using a computer and the World Wide Web.
- I will not give my address or my telephone number without permission.
- I will not give my school's name and address without permission.
- I will say 'No' if anyone who I've met on the World Wide Web wants to meet me, unless my parent(s)/guardian(s) have agreed and will go with me.
- I won't put my photograph on a web site.
- I will tell my parent(s)/guardian(s) or teacher if I discover something on the World Wide Web which worries or upsets me.

With thanks to the Girl Scouts of the USA for the initial ideas contained in this warning for children.

Photographs Diana Aynaci

Contents

Remember to open the time capsule you made from the 1999 Brownie Annual!

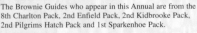

The Brownie Guides who appear in this Annual are from the 8th Charlton Pack, 2nd Enfield Pack, 2nd Kidbrooke Pack, 2nd Pilgrims Hatch Pack and 1st Sparkenhoe Pack.

Special thanks to: Lucy Farmer and Nicola Brewerton at the WWF-UK (Fight For Life!): Chris Lawrence, Tessa Bailey and Amanda Bailey at the RSPCA (Pet Rabbit): Tessa Bailey and Emma Nutbrown at the RSPCA, Rainforest Cafe, Steven Blows at Review Travel and the Guide Heritage Centre (Wild Animal Adventure): Sally and Peter Mitchell at Orchid Veterinary Surgery and the RSPB for supplying bird feeders (I'm Bored!): Jane Murray at The Forestry Commission (Growing Planet): May Leung at NEXT PLC (Tempting Trendy Togs).

Stars On Your Sky text compiled by Brenda Apsley: Is Anyone Out There?, Chinese Challenger!, Keep Fit In A Minute, Against The Clock!, On The Ball!, 2000 Good Turns, Fit For The Olympics!, Don't Waste It, In The Zone, A Star Turn!, Great Games, Hop Till You Drop, Millennium World!, Back To The Future, Space Snacks, Olympic Feats, Planet-saver, Party Pick And Mix and Round The World! text

compiled by Liz Bussey: Football Flowers text compiled by Liz Duffey: It's A First, Down Under, Getting Greener, Costing The Earth and The Ultimate Party text compiled by Jenny Wackett: Super Brownie And The Millennium Party written by Marion Thompson: I'm Bored! written by Jenny Wackett.

All Brownie Guide photographs by Diana Aynaci. Freda illustrated by Bill Ledger.

2000 Brownie Annual
© The Guide Association 1999

Photographs © as acknowledged in features: all other photographs © The Guide Association: 'Miss Jones' (approximately 1,600, pp 57–71) from RATS ON THE ROOF AND OTHER STORIES by James Marshall (Puffin, 1991), copyright © James Marshall, 1991, reprinted by permission of Penguin Books Ltd: illustrations for 'Miss Jones' © Haydn Cornner: 'The All-Purpose Children's Poem' (p 76, 20 lines) from PILLOW TALK by Roger McGough (Viking, 1990), copyright © Roger McGough, 1990, reprinted by permission of Penguin Books Ltd.

Published by The Guide Association (a registered charity), 17–19 Buckingham Palace Road, London SW1W 0PT
E-mail: chq@guides.org.uk Web site: www.guides.org.uk

An official publication of The Guide Association (incorporated by Royal Charter)
registered charity number 306016
ISBN 0 85260 155 7
The Guide Association Trading Service ordering code 60053

Brownie Guide Adviser Susan Jones (until 1998) and Sandra Moffit (from 1999): Project Editor Alice Forbes: Publications Manager Anne Moffat: Studio Gillian Webb, Joanne Harkness, David Jones, Caroline Marklew, Cathy Summers: Editorial Rebecca Davis, Annabelle Mundy and Helen Sutcliffe: Production Richard Dickerson-Watts: Colour repro by Valhaven Limited: Printed and bound in Belgium by Proost NV.

Readers are reminded that during the life span of this publication, there may be changes to The Guide Association's policy, or legal requirements, that will affect the accuracy of information contained within these pages.

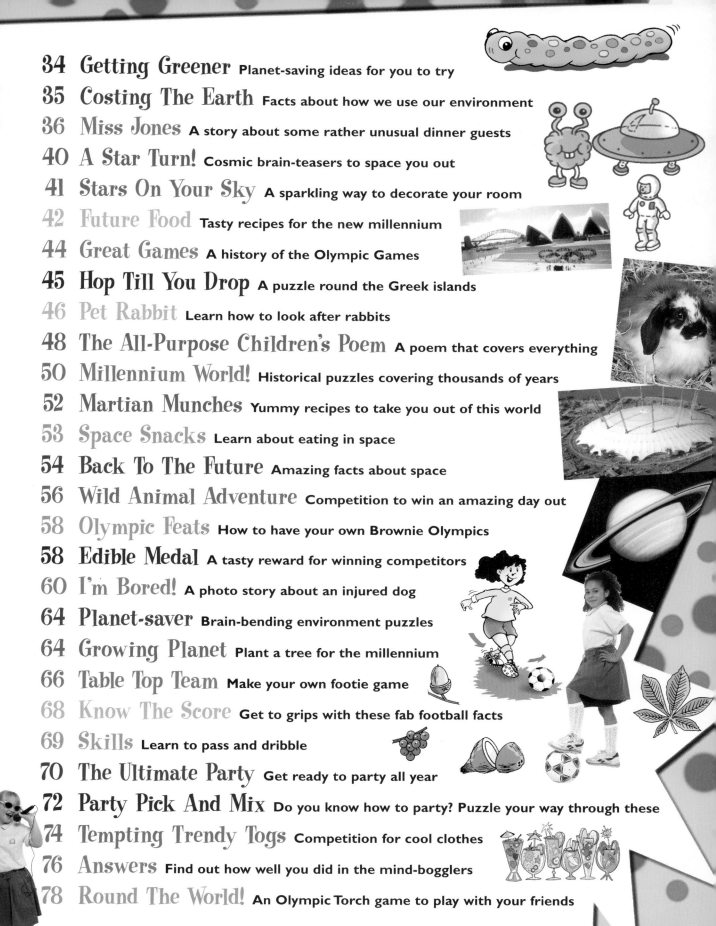

All illustrations and photographs as acknowledged on appropriate pages.

Dragon

Have a fiery feast to start the Chinese year of the Dragon in February with these red and flaming foods!

Dragons

1. Thinly slice the carrot. Cut the ends into ribbons. Place in cold water.

2. Rinse the celery, then trim and dry it. Cut each cheese triangle in half. Put the cheese in the celery.

3. Cut the pepper into long slices. Stick two bits in the cheese at one end to make the tail.

Ingredients
pack of celery ★ cheese spread
triangles ★ red pepper
★ few red grapes ★ carrot
★ paprika (optional)

You need
knife ★ chopping board
★ bowl of cold water
★ kitchen paper

Illustrations Bill Ledger

Chinese Challenger!

Tackle these brain teasers!

Illustrations Tom Clayton

Enter the dragon
Spot 12 differences between the dancing dragons.

Feasts

BADGE WORK

4 Cut the red grapes in half and take out any pips. Place two halves on the other end as eyes.

5 When the carrots have curled, stick one in the mouth.

⚠ Ask a grown-up to help in the kitchen.

Get your chops round that! For an extra-fierce dragon sprinkle a little paprika on it!

Tasty toast
Start your day with an extra zing!

Ingredients
slice of hot toast
★ butter or margarine
★ pinch of cinnamon
★ ½ teaspoon sugar

You need
teaspoon ★ knife
★ plate

Go easy on the cinnamon for me!

Mix the cinnamon and sugar. Spread the toast with loads of butter. Sprinkle on the sugar mix. Tuck in!

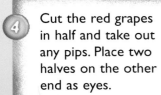

Message finder
Find the special message written Chinese fashion!

```
M R V O O T I B
Y F E I A T S R
A U M N N H T O
N N O G D I H W
N W N T I N E N
U I S O A G B I
A T T H M I E E
L H E A G D S S
```

Mind-bogglers

Light riddles
The Chinese write riddles on lanterns during their Lantern Festival.
My first is in red but not in green.
My second is at the start of rice.
My third is in panda, tea and bamboo.
There's two of my fourth in ginger
There's oodles of my fifth in a noodle.
My sixth appears twice in lantern.
2000 is my year. I am a _ _ _ _ _ _ _.

Fight For Life!

Here in Europe a fight for survival is going on. Lynxes, wolves and brown bears are struggling for their lives.

Iberian lynx

Like the tiger, the lynx is called a big cat. Only a small number of Iberian lynx are found in small parts of Spain and Portugal. There are less than 800 left and it is the world's most endangered cat species. One reason is because lynx eat a lot of rabbit. There aren't many rabbits left because man and disease have killed them off.

Pablo Ferreras

Grey wolf

Wolves used to live all over Europe, but now there are only a few places they can be found. Some people don't like wolves close to them. It is important they are helped to understand that wolves aren't any more dangerous than a pet dog! Wolves are very shy and intelligent animals.

Christoph Promberger

Bear and wolf

Bear and wolf

Bear and wolf

Wolf

Lynx

Wolf

Bear and wolf

Mountain High Maps® Copyright © 1993 Digital Wisdom, Inc.

Christoph Promberger

Bear sleep

In some places bears have become nocturnal. This means they sleep during the day and come out at night. This is because humans attack them, or make it hard for them to live during the day.

Brown bears love to sleep. From late in the autumn to springtime they hibernate, which is a really long sleep. They hibernate in a large hole in the ground or under rocks where they won't be found easily.

Eating habits

A carnivore is an animal that eats only meat. Lynxes and wolves are carnivores. Brown bears are omnivores which means they eat meat and vegetables. Just like most humans, in fact! There are no longer any large carnivores living in the United Kingdom. There are some small ones like the otter, pine marten, polecat, fox and badger.

Brown bear

Brown bears are huge animals and can weigh between 140 kilograms and 320 kilograms. That's about four to eight Brownies! They eat a mix of things from nuts and fruit to insects and meat. They don't kill many animals themselves. Usually any meat they eat is another animal's leftovers.

Christoph Promberger

Nowhere to live

Humans have destroyed many forests and also hunt these creatures. The animals that the lynxes, wolves and bears ate also disappeared with the forests. Without safe homes and food to eat these animals won't come back. Once they are back it is important that people leave them alone.

Visit the WWF-UK website on www.wwf-uk.org

WWF campaign

The World Wide Fund for Nature's Campaign for Europe's Carnivores aims to help lynxes, wolves and brown bears so they can carry on living in Europe. To find out more, or to get involved, contact WWF-UK, Panda House, Weyside Park, Catteshall Lane, Godalming, Surrey GU7 1XR.

WWF

With thanks to WWF for their help with this feature.

Keep Fit In A Minute

Get into the new millennium with a keep-fit promise to yourself. Have a go at these great Brownie round-the-world exercises with your mates.

Clock how well you do

You'll need a watch or clock. One with a second hand is best. How many times can you do each exercise in two minutes?

On your marks

Don't wear jewellery. Choose loose, comfy clothes. Tie back long hair.

Warm and stretch

March on the spot.
Touch your toes.
Reach for the clouds.

Get set and go!

Stand up straight with feet slightly apart. Relax.

 Stop if an exercise hurts. If you have back or knee pains don't try any of these activities.

Leaping British puddles

Take one big step with your right foot. Step back. Repeat with your left foot.

Your routine

Do the exercises two or three times each week. Keep counting how many can you do in two minutes. Are you managing more each time? Keep a note here.

Week	1		2		3		4		5	
Write in the day										
Leaping British puddles										
American star										
Nepal mountain										
Eiffel Tower										
Canadian skiing										
Chinese cycle										
Dutch canals										

American star

Jump high. Make a star!

Nepal mountain

Right hand and left leg high. Pull down. Now left hand and right foot. Like climbing a rope.

Eiffel Tower

Step up onto something strong and solid. Right foot first for ten, then left foot first.

Canadian skiing

Feet together. Jump up and twist. Land facing the other way. Back again. Really fast!

Chinese cycle

Cycle with your legs. No free-wheeling! Try going backwards.

Dutch canals

Keep your left hand still. Move your right in a big circle. Now hold your right hand still and move your left.

Cool off

Gently repeat the warm-up. Let your muscles relax.

Photographs Diana Aynaci

Mind-bogglers

Against The Clock!

Be a couch-potato with this fitness puzzle.

Be a sport. Find these fit words in the word ball!

jog	canoe	squash	football
row	dance	tennis	rounders
run	rugby	cricket	softball
ski	ballet	fencing	badminton
swim	diving	netball	volleyball
walk	hockey	baseball	

```
        C L O C
      S R E D N U O R
    R K U N E T B A L L
   I T U N F O O T B A L L
  G E N G H S A U Q S A L
 W N K B E B O M E S G B A U
 O I C A P O Y C I K S Y B A
 R C I L W I N N K W N E E N
 I N R L N A N A G E S L S T
 E C E D E I M C E Y L A
 F W T T G N I V I D O B
  B A D M I N T O N V
   L L A B T F O S
      K G O J
```

Once you've found all the words discover the hidden sporting message. Start at the top left and write each letter in the boxes below.

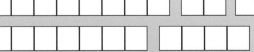

Did you sprint to the end? Find out if you're a winner on page 76.

Illustrations Tom Clayton

The Cow

The friendly cow, all red and white,
I love with all my heart:
She gives me cream with all her might,
To eat with apple tart.

Illustration Kate Wells

14

She wanders lowing here and there,
And yet she cannot stray,
All in the pleasant open air,
The pleasant light of day;

And blown by all the winds that pass
And wet with all the showers,
She walks among the meadow grass
And eats the meadow flowers.

Robert Louis Stevenson 1850–1894

On The Ball!

Kick off Euro 2000 with these winning games!

Hot shots!
Which player scored the goal?

Football crazy
Spot the soccer star who's from another team.

National players

Match the items from each country.
Write the numbers in the boxes.

England   France   Netherlands   Scotland   Italy

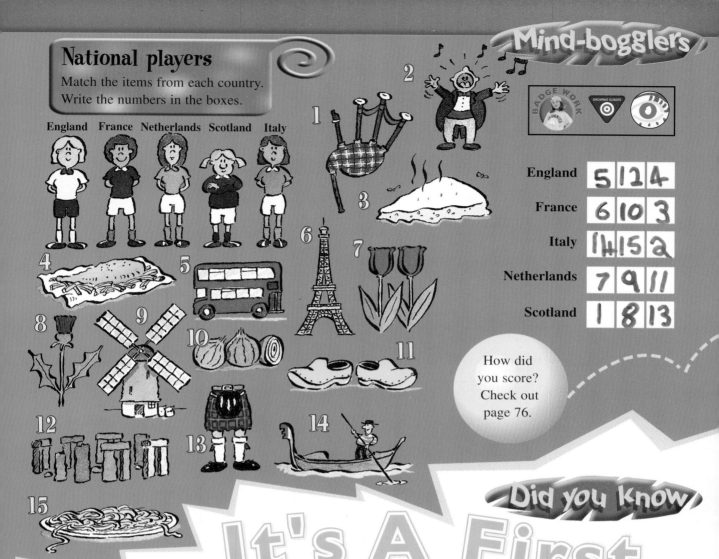

England	5	2	4
France	6	10	3
Italy	14	15	2
Netherlands	7	9	11
Scotland	1	8	13

How did you score? Check out page 76.

Did you know

It's A First

Belgium and the Netherlands are hosts of Euro 2000! It's the first time the European Cup is being held in two countries.

Belgium

Football and cycling are the most popular sports in Belgium. On Sunday afternoons cycle races take place in most towns.

Cafés are a favourite place to meet friends. Belgians love to drink coffee and eat tasty cakes called pastries.

Belgium is famous for really yummy chocolate, too.

Brussels is the capital of Belgium, and also its largest city.

The Netherlands

Much of the Netherlands was once under the sea. The land has been drained and big walls called dykes keep the water out. The land is really flat, and there are a lot of canals.

People in the Netherlands like some strange sports. They hold ice-skating races on the canals in the winter when they freeze solid. Pole-vaulting over dykes is also a favourite! Football, sailing, cycling and swimming are the sports most people do, though!

The Netherlands is famous for tulips, windmills and clogs. It has two big cities, Rotterdam and Amsterdam.

Trip/TH-Foto Werbung

I'll be watching the final of Euro 2000 on 2nd July!

17

The Netherlands, host country of football extravaganza Euro 2000, is famous for tulips and daffodils. Get into yellow and red with these bright and breezy ideas.

Football

Daffodil waste

You need
small waste paper bin ★ tape measure
★ yellow paper ★ thin yellow card ★
glue or sticky tape ★ scissors

1 Cover the bin with yellow paper. Then measure the distance round the bin and also it's height.

+20cm

+5cm

2 Cut a piece of yellow card 5cm longer and 20cm deeper than the bin. Make five evenly spaced cuts.

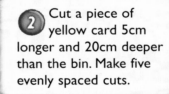

3 Fix the card round the bin. Cut the flaps into petal shapes. Bend them back a bit.

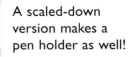

A scaled-down version makes a pen holder as well!

Illustrations Frances Lloyd

Flowers

1 Mix a tablespoon of flour with a little water to make a thin paste. Mix in the yellow food colouring. Paint some of the cake cases. Make another paste with the red colouring. Wash the brush well, then paint some cases red.

Millennium bug

You need

fairy cake cases ★ few drops of yellow and red food colouring ★ flour ★ clean paint brush ★ water ★ icing sugar ★ marzipan coated in jam ★ marshmallows ★ dolly mix ★ colourful chocolate sweets ★ liquorice laces and shapes

2 Make sugar glue from a tablespoon of icing sugar, adding a tiny bit of water. Use this or the jam to stick the sweets together to make your own millennium bug!

Tulip tops

You need

colourful felt ★ scissors ★ needle and thread ★ pen ★ green tape ★ glue

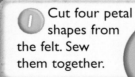

1 Cut four petal shapes from the felt. Sew them together.

Be clever and add green felt leaves as you wind.

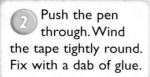

2 Push the pen through. Wind the tape tightly round. Fix with a dab of glue.

19

Down Under

The 2000 Olympic Games are happening in Sydney, Australia this summer. Watch out for them from 15 September to 1 October!

Odd birds

Cassowaries can't fly and have curious shaggy feathers. Once the female lays her eggs, the male hatches them and brings up the young.

Oxford Scientific Films/Steve Turner

Upside down

Australia is right on the other side of the planet. Things there can seem weird if you're used to the United Kingdom. Winter is in June and July, with summer in December and January. Even the stars are different, like the Southern Cross on their flag that never appears here.

Dry, wet and hot

The very north is tropical, with just two seasons. One is hot and dry, the other is hot and wet! The middle of the country is really dry. It barely rains at all and there are huge deserts.

Barbecued Bangers

You need
wooden cocktail sticks ★ oven gloves ★ tongs

Summer sizzle, or camp cook-out. Give this great Aussie-style tucker a go!

Little pig in a blanket

1 Wrap a rasher round each sausage. Secure with a cocktail stick. Toss them on the barbecue.

Ingredients
★ 6 thin sausages
★ 6 bacon rashers
★ 6 finger bread rolls
★ tomato ketchup or other sauces

2 Turn them with tongs so they cook right through and the bacon is nice and crispy. Take them off and let them cool a little.

3 Cut or tear open the rolls. Take out the cocktail sticks, put a sausage with bacon inside each roll.

4 Splash on the ketchup and get stuck in!

⚠ Ask a grown-up to help you. Never light or cook on a barbecue without adult help.

Illustrations Stephanie Strickland

Did you know

Amazing animals

Australia is home to some of the world's oddest creatures. Kangaroos and wombats are marsupials. This means they give birth to their babies in a pouch on their belly. Mothers carry their babies round until they can look after themselves.

Oxford Scientific Films/Kathie Atkinson

Even stranger are echidnas. They and platypuses are the only animals left in the world that are monotremes – that's a mammal that lays eggs. Mammals include humans, cows and cats, but not fish, lizards, birds or insects.

Oxford Scientific Films/Daniel J Fox

Oxford Scientific Films/Michael Silver

Biggest barrier

The Great Barrier Reef is 2,000 kilometres long and 80 kilometres wide in places (London to Edinburgh is only 600 kilometres!). It is the longest coral reef in the world. Most of the reef is about two million years old, but some of it goes back 18 million years.

Get stuck in

Sweet dreams

You need
knife ★ cooking foil ★ oven gloves

Open the parcel and let it cool. If it's raining, cook these in the oven.

Peel the potatoes and chop into chunks. Cut the onions into quarters. Place the potatoes and onion on a square of foil with a big knob of butter. Fold the foil and pinch the edges. Cook for 30 to 40 minutes.

Ingredients
sweet or normal potatoes ★ onions ★ butter, margarine or oil

Aussie fact file
Capital Canberra
Currency Australian dollar and cents
Language English
Australia Day 26 January

Visit the Guides Australia web site at www.guidesaus.org.au

2000 Good

A tough challenge! Can you top 2000 Good Turns to start the millennium?

 Remember to check things with a grown-up before you start!

Your law

You're bound to be doing your Good Turn every day. Here's a challenge to top 2000 for this special year. Are you up to it? You'll need a little help from your friends.

Team effort

You'd have to be an extra-special Brownie to do 2000 Good Turns by yourself! Call on the rest of your Six to help out. For starters you each need to make sure you do one every day. That's already a lot, but to be on the safe side you'll have to fit in some extra special ones. Get stuck into some of these smart ideas.

Every day

Put fresh water out for your pet. Clean your teeth. Make your bed. Unstack the dishwasher and put everything away. Smile instead of frowning.

Each week

Sort the papers for recycling. Help mop the kitchen floor. Clean your bike till it sparkles! Help unpack the shopping. Put your clothes away. Clean your pet's cage. Vacuum inside the car. Water the plants. Keep your Six corner tidy at Brownies.

You and your Six

Write to Brownies in another country. Help tidy away at the end of Brownies. Make sure a new Brownie knows all about Freda. Go to a Guide meeting and tell your Pack about it!

Turns

Special days

Pick a day that's special for you and do something to make it really fun for someone else. Check out these for starters. **Leap Day** is 29th February. Spend this whole extra day tidying your room! Make an extra-nice filling for a friend's pancakes on **Pancake Day**. Make a trendy card for your **best mate's birthday**. Help hang the **Christmas** decs, or stick the stamps on the card envelopes. For **Bonfire Night** on 5th November make sure your pet has a quiet night. Send a message to a Brownie in another country on the Internet for **Thinking Day** on 22nd February. Think up a **New Year's Day** resolution for 1st January – and keep it! Send a **Valentine's Day** card to someone nice for 14th February. Wear bright clothes for **Holi**, the festival of colour, in March.

Check out pages 34–35 for some great planet-saving Good Turns!

Seasonal specials

Winter Help clear ice and snow outside your Brownie meeting place. Put out food and water each day for the birds. Start a keep-fit routine with your friends. **Spring** Do a nice April Fool's surprise on a friend. Make breakfast in bed for someone special – with some grown-up help, of course! Spring-clean your bedroom! **Summer** Say thanks to your teacher for a great year. Look after a friend's pet when she's on holiday. Help a new Brownie have fun at camp or holiday. **Autumn** Get into a good habit of doing your homework every day – yuk! Plant bulbs for a colourful spring. Make and send a Diwali card to a friend.

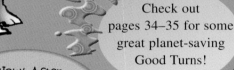

Wow! After all that I need a lie-down!

Keep counting!

Make a special Good Turn book. Draw pictures and stick in photos of all the Good Turns you do. Make sure you write down all the ones you do with your Six. You may even get 'thank you' letters to stick in!

Illustrations Nick Diggory

23

It's all ready for the night!

Wow! It looks great.

Remember the food.

MILLENNIU

Oh no! We forgot the clock.

I think there's going to be a special suprise.

Our little Big Ben has a radio inside. We'll hear the New Year chimes.

Wow!

PPY MILLEN

The next evening...

That's all the food.

Let's get going or we'll be late.

Wait till I get my hat.

I'll just turn the car round.

Wait! I haven't tied it on. Oh no!

How will the Brownies know when it's midnight? Turn over to find out!

Fit For The

An action-packed 2000 Olympic Games takes place down under in Australia this summer. Don't miss out on the fun with these brain-bending puzzles!

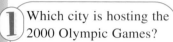

Olympic trivia

Find out how much you know about the Olympics with this quiz.

1 Which city is hosting the 2000 Olympic Games?
a Rome
b New York
c Sydney

2 How many sports will there be at the Games?
a 24
b 30
c 28

3 How often does the Olympics take place?
a Every 3 years
b Every 4 years
c Every 5 years

4 How do the Olympic Games start?
a With a torch
b With an arrow
c With fireworks

5 What's the Olympic symbol?
a Five rings
b A picture of a runner
c An olive wreath medal

6 Who competes in the Paralympics?
a Athletes with a disability
b Elderly athletes
c Children

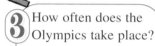
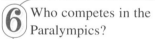

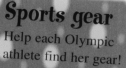

Sports gear

Help each Olympic athlete find her gear!

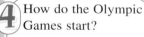

Olympics!

What a ball!
How many balls can you find?

Ride on
Help the rider find a clear round over five fences to win the gold medal!

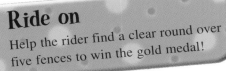

The Olympic flag was first flown at the 1920 Games in Belgium!

Did you win a gold? Sprint to page 76 to find out!

Good Time

This amazing clock was used in ancient Egypt. Does it stand the test of time? Make your own and see how to measure minutes.

Ancient cups

The Egyptians used stone bowls with spouts not plastic cups!

You need

2 polystyrene or plastic cups
★ paint and brushes ★ darning needle
★ 1 piece of wood about 20cm x 15cm
★ 1 piece of dowling about 30cm long
★ plasticine ★ wood glue ★ sticky tape
★ jug of water ★ pencil
★ a watch with a second hand

1 Decorate both cups and make a hole in the bottom of one. Glue the dowling in place and secure with a ring of plasticine.

 Ask a grown-up for help.

2 Stick the cup with the hole to the dowling. Place the other cup under it. Cover the hole with your finger. Fill the cup with water.

Don't Waste It

Think you've got too much of it? Can't get enough? It's not all a waste of time! Have a go at these time-saving tips.

Undo the laces on your trainers when you take them off.

When your shampoo's running out, leave the bottle standing upside down. Careful when you open it, though!

Stick photos in an album as soon as you get them. Write next to each one what it is, who's in it and add the date.

Ticking ideas

Buy a clock mechanism from a craft shop and create your own wondrous millennium timekeeper!

3 When a new minute starts take your finger away and start timing. Every minute mark the water level. It is easier to see and mark the level on the inside of the cup.

4 Double check the clock is accurate by filling the top cup with water. Time how long it takes the water level to reach each notch again. Is it exactly one minute?

Illustrations Bill Ledger

Now try this

At Brownie camp, stack all the washing-up in the right order. Glasses first, then plates and lastly knives, forks, pots and pans.

Hang up your clothes, or stack them away so they're crumple-free when you need them next.

Get out of bed the first time you're asked!

Take a peek at page 22 for more great ideas.

Ask a grown-up you live with how you can help them save time. It may be your Good Turn for the day!

31

Did you think you were sitting still? Well find out about time zones and know that you're not! Take a spin round your planet.

Same time

Take a look at what's going on round the world. All the times shown are happening at once.

Time zone

The world is divided into 24 time zones, one for every hour of the day. Each day starts and stops on the International Date Line that runs through the Pacific Ocean. The Greenwich Mean Line, that runs through London, is 12 hours behind. So midnight on the Date Line, is noon in London.

Mexico

This Fairy visiting Our Cabaña will take part in a candlelit ceremony round the swimming pool. Our Cabaña is a world Guiding centre.

Sun rise, new day

The Earth spins round so different parts of it face the sun at different times. As the sun rises over the UK it leaves Asia in darkness. As the sun sets here a new day is starting in America.

Greenwich Mean Line

Kiribati

These tiny islands are one of the first places to start a new day and the new millennium! These Brownies are in bed now, but had fun during the day.

International Date Line

Kiribati Sheila Mathieson: Mexico WAGGGS: UK The Guide Association/Diana Aynaci: Russia Oxford Scientific Films/Richard and Julia Kemp: Sangam The Guide Association: Elephant and truck Oxford Scientific Films/Ajay Desai: South Africa The Guide Association

Zone

UK
The Brownies are enjoying lunch!

Russia
These children are going sledging. It's quite cold!

India
Guiding has a world centre here called Sangam which means 'joining together'.

Have an extra-special millennium Thinking Day party!

South Africa
These Brownies have been to the beach for a swim to cool down. As they leave, they say 'hamba kahle' (hum-ba garsh lee) which means 'go well' in Zulu.

Thinking Day
Thinking Day on 22nd February is like a special Guiding birthday. Brownies all over the world think of one another.

33

Getting Greener

Planet Earth is fragile. What are you doing to help it last another millennium? Here are some easy ways to look after your planet.

TRIP/H Rogers

Use it again

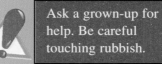

Don't just throw away something that could be used in another way. If you can't use it, someone else might be able to. Find out where there are recycling bins near you. There are usually bins for glass, metals, paper and clothes. Sort your rubbish then pop each lot into the right bin. Give things you don't want any more to charity shops. Make sure they are clean and not broken.

> Ask a grown-up for help. Be careful touching rubbish.

Don't let it go

A radiator warms your room by sending heat out from all its sides. Heat comes out of the back as well as the front and can be lost in the wall. Cover a sheet of card with silver foil and put it between the wall and the radiator. This makes the heat bounce back into the room.

★ Close doors to keep the cold air out and the heat in.
★ Close curtains when it's dark and cold outside to keep the heat in.
★ Stop draughts from under doors with this excluder.

You need
110cm x 15cm material
★ needle and thread ★
20cm string ★ safety pin
★ old tights chopped up
★ felt, buttons and odd
bits of material

 1 Turn one short edge over and sew. Use the pin to thread the string through.

2 Sew the long edges together and the other short edge. Tie both ends of the string.

3 Turn it inside out and stuff with chopped tights. Draw the string tight and knot.

 4 Give it a face or decorate it, if you want.

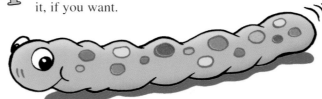

Illustrations Nick Diggory

Switch it off!

Some electricity is made by burning coal. So even if you can't see it, lots of smoke and chemicals go into the air. Not using as much electricity means the air is cleaner. It also means the electricity bill is less! Try these ones out.

Oxford Scientific Films/Kim Westerskov

★ Switch the telly off. Don't leave it on stand-by.

★ Only boil as much water as you need for the tea.

★ Last one out of a room switches off the light.

Did you know

Costing The Earth

Are you wasting this planet? Or are you doing something about turning it around?

Oxford Scientific Films/Niall Benvie

Waste tip

The average family throws away 1.5 tonnes of rubbish a year! That's like throwing away half an elephant! Every year Britain throws away enough rubbish to cover 60 football pitches with piles of waste as high as a mountain.

Paper weight

Seven million tonnes of paper and card are used every year. Two million tonnes are recycled. Five million tonnes are just thrown away! To make those five million tonnes, 65 million trees have been cut down. That's like two whole rainforests.

Take a look at www.wastewatch.org.uk

TRIP/Viesti Associates

TRIP/C Moncrieff

Miss Jones

by James Marshall

Miss Jones had just settled down to a mug of milky tea and a plate of biscuits, when the telephone rang.

"I might have known," she complained. "Someone always calls when I'm having treats."

Miss Jones waddled over to the telephone and picked up the receiver.

"Hello," she said, somewhat irritably.

"Well?" said her friend Rose, who lived in the building. "What are they like, your new neighbours across the hall in 12E? The postman said a couple moved in during the night."

"I haven't heard a thing," said Miss Jones, "but my hearing isn't what it used to be."

"I'm dying to know what they look like," said Rose. "Why don't you peek out into the hall and see what you can see?"

"You know how dark the hall is," said Miss Jones, "and besides, my eyesight isn't so good. I can't see my beak in front of my face."

"Well as soon as you hear anything at all, give me a call," said Rose. And she hung up.

Miss Jones nibbled on her biscuits and sipped her milky tea.

"New neighbours," she said. "I do hope we get along."

When she had finished her snack, she took the dishes into the kitchen to wash up.

"Moving is such hard work," she said, "I think I'll heat up some vegetable soup and take it over. That will be a friendly gesture."

When the soup was ready, Miss Jones stepped across the hall. It took her some time to locate the bell.

"Who is it?" called out a deep female voice.

"It is Miss Jones from across the hall," said Miss Jones. "I've brought you some vegetable soup."

The door of 12E opened, but just a crack.

Miss Jones could not see the long furry nose protruding out, or the long, sharp white teeth.

"I thought you might be too tired to cook," said Miss Jones.

"We *can't* cook yet," said the new neighbour. "The gas company hasn't turned on the gas. Otherwise…"

"Well then," said Miss Jones, holding out the pot of soup, "I hope you will enjoy this."

"Thanks," said the new neighbour.

Miss Jones squinted and stepped closer to the open door.

"I really can't see you very well," she said, "this hallway is so dark."

"My husband and I are canaries," said the new neighbour quickly.

"Oh, how lovely," said Miss Jones. "But you don't sound like canaries."

"We have low voices," said the neighbour.

"But we *are* canaries," said a deep male voice from behind the door. "We are the Carusos."

"I'm so pleased to meet you," said Miss Jones. "When you are all settled in, we must get together for dinner."

The Carusos both gasped.

"By all means!" said Mrs Caruso. "We'd like nothing better."

"I'll be off now," said Miss Jones. "Toodleloo."

"Toodleloo," said the Carusos.

Miss Jones went inside her apartment. Charming couple, she thought.

Mrs Caruso closed the door to 12E. "If only that stove had been working!" she said.

That evening Miss Jones consulted her calendar.

"My stars," she said. "Christmas is only two days away. I really must start planning my big Christmas dinner."

But then she remembered that this Christmas her friend Rose would be out of town visiting her family.

"It will be a lonely Christmas indeed," said Miss Jones. "But I'll make the best of it."

The doorbell rang.

"Who is it?" called out Miss Jones, who never opened the door without knowing who was on the other side.

"It is I, Mrs Caruso," said the new neighbour.

Miss Jones threw open the door. "Do come in," she said.

"I only have a minute," said Mrs Caruso, remaining in the dark hall. "My husband and I were hoping you'd join us for Christmas dinner. It would give us such pleasure."

Miss Jones was thrilled.

"I should be delighted!" she exclaimed. "May I bring anything?"

"Just yourself," said Mrs Caruso, and she hurried back into her own apartment.

"What a lovely surprise," said Miss Jones, closing and bolting her door.

The next morning the telephone rang.

"Well?" said Rose. "Have you met them yet?"

"Oh yes," said Miss Jones. "They are delightful. Canaries, you know. And they have invited me for Christmas dinner."

"Marvellous," said Rose. "Now I don't have to worry about you being all alone."

No sooner had Miss Jones hung up the telephone than it rang again.

It was Mrs Caruso. "I hate to bother you, my dear," she said, "but do you by any chance have a nice big roasting pan? Ours seems to have been lost in the move."

"Why certainly," said Miss Jones. "Is there anything else you need?"

"As a matter of fact," said Mrs Caruso, "would you know a good recipe for plum sauce?"

"I surely do," replied Miss Jones. "And why don't you allow me to make it? I'd so love to contribute to the dinner."

"If you like," said Mrs Caruso.

There was a short pause.

"I *do* hope I don't ruin the wild rice again this year," said Mrs Caruso.

Miss Jones insisted on preparing the wild rice as well. "I'd be happy to do it," she said. "You just concentrate on the main course."

"Oh we will," said Mrs Caruso.

Miss Jones felt it would be impolite to ask what the main course would be. "I'm sure it will be tasty."

On Christmas Eve Mrs Caruso called again with a slight problem.

"The gas company still hasn't turned on the stove," she said. "I don't know *what* we're going to do!"

Miss Jones had the solution immediately.

"But you must use mine," she said.

"You are kind. What would we do without you?" said Mrs Caruso. "Have the oven good and hot about noon."

"We can have eggnog while we're waiting for dinner," said Miss Jones.

Mrs Caruso thought this was an excellent idea, although she confessed that eggnog was really not one of her specialities.

On Christmas morning the Carusos were up bright and early.

"This is going to be a Christmas to remember!" said Mr Caruso.

"Yum, yum, yum!" said his wife. "I hope there will be plenty of plum sauce."

In her own apartment, Miss Jones, who had got up even earlier, was merrily setting the table.

"I have such pretty china," she said.

At noon on the nose, the Carusos rang the doorbell, and Miss Jones opened the door.

"Merry Christmas!" she said.

"Merry Christmas!" said the Carusos, stepping inside. "Is the oven nice and hot?"

"Oh dear, oh dear," said Miss Jones. "I *knew* I'd forget something."

The Carusos were quite put out, but they tried not to show it.

"No harm done," said Mrs Caruso. "Turn it on right now. We'll start on the eggnog."

Miss Jones went into the kitchen and came back shortly.

"It won't take long to heat up," she said.

"Good," said the Carusos.

Conversation did not flow easily.

"Nice day," said Mr Caruso.

"Very nice indeed," said Miss Jones, "and so lovely to share it with new neighbours."

"Yes," said the Carusos.

"I think I'll go see about the oven," said Mrs Caruso, and she got up to go into the kitchen. Suddenly Miss Jones felt a long furry tail brush up against her feet as Mrs Caruso passed.

Oh no, thought Miss Jones, the Carusos aren't canaries at all!

And right away she saw what was up.

"Miss Jones, dear," Mrs Caruso called out from the kitchen. "Would you step in here a minute?"

Miss Jones knew she had to do some fast talking—or else!

"I'm sure you can take care of everything," she answered back. "You don't need me. Come have another cup of eggnog."

Mrs Caruso returned.

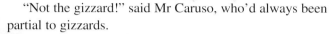

"The oven is ready," she said, giving her husband a significant look.

"I'm sure I won't be able to eat more than a few bites," said Miss Jones. "Ever since my operation I haven't had much appetite."

"Operation?" said the Carusos.

"Actually, I've had several," said Miss Jones. "They took out my gizzard."

"Not the gizzard!" said Mr Caruso, who'd always been partial to gizzards.

"And I have only a tiny bit of my liver left," said Miss Jones. "Hardly anything at all."

"That's really too bad!" said the Carusos.

"Of course," said Miss Jones, "my doctor does want me to put on weight. I'm just a bag of bones."

"You look pretty plump to me," said Mrs Caruso.

"Feathers," said Miss Jones. "Merely feathers, very deceptive."

The Carusos could now see their big Christmas dinner vanishing before their very eyes.

Miss Jones began to scratch frantically.

"Do excuse me," she said. "I know it's rude to do this in company, but I have such a flea problem."

"You don't say," said the Carusos.

Miss Jones continued.

"Of course," she said, "I'm not implying I don't have absolute faith in my doctor, but I do wish he wouldn't give me all that medicine. I'm positively *stuffed* with milk of magnesia."

Now this was simply too much for the Carusos, and they hastily made their excuses.

"We hate to run off like this," said Mr Caruso, "but we forgot we always visit house-bound people at Christmas."

Miss Jones did not insist on their staying.

"We'll get together in the new year," she said.

"Of course," said the Carusos (if that was their real name), and they hurried off, hoping to find *something* decent to eat for Christmas.

"You and your bright ideas!" mumbled Mr Caruso.

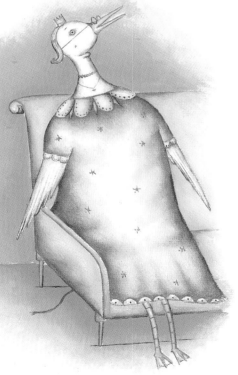

Miss Jones bolted the door, collapsed on the sofa, and heaved great sighs of relief. Then she placed a call to her landlord, who was shocked to learn he had wolves in the building.

"I shall remedy this situation immediately, Miss Jones," he said.

Miss Jones felt reassured and vowed to open her door to no one until she was advised that the Carusos had departed for good.

That night she sat down to a big plate of plum sauce.

"I really shouldn't," she said. "My doctor says I'm a little overweight, but sometimes we need to reward ourselves."

And she ate it all.

'Miss Jones' (approximately 1,600, pp 57–71) from RATS ON THE ROOF AND OTHER STORIES by James Marshall (Puffin, 1991) Copyright © James Marshall, 1991. Reprinted by permission of Penguin Books Ltd.

Illustrations Haydn Cornner

A Star Turn!

Is there life on Mars? Do aliens really exist? They do in these space puzzles!

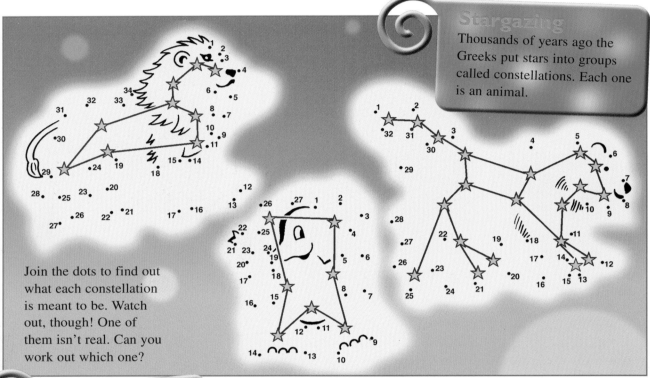

Illustrations Kevin Jones Associates

Stargazing

Thousands of years ago the Greeks put stars into groups called constellations. Each one is an animal.

Join the dots to find out what each constellation is meant to be. Watch out, though! One of them isn't real. Can you work out which one?

Space to base

Work out what these alien messages say!

be a

to be

Brownie?

a very

Earth is

special

your

I'd like

Can I

friend!

planet!

MESSAGE

40

Alien invasion
The aliens have gathered for a race. Get them to their spaceships and to their homes!

Blast off to page 76 to see how well you did!

Stars On Your Sky

These stars are sure to shine on your bedroom ceiling.

Get stuck in

You need
thin card ★ pencil ★ scissors ★ glue ★ silver hologram paper or kitchen foil ★ double-sided sticky tape or normal tape

1 Draw star shapes onto your card. Cut them out.

2 Glue each star to the silver paper. Carefully cut round them.

3 Cut little bits of double-sided tape. Stick them to the back of the stars.

4 Decide what pattern you are going to make with your stars. Ask a tall person to help you stick them in place.

⚠ Check it's OK to stick things to the ceiling!

Illustrations Bill Ledger

41

Future Food

Get your mates to try out these great tastes for the new millennium. They're the yummiest treats you'll eat all year!

QA Photos Ltd

Ingredients
tub of vanilla ice-cream ★ your favourite ice-cream ★ chocolate chips or dolly mixture ★ 12 chocolate fingers

Dome surprise

You need
glass bowl ★ oil ★ brush ★ cling film ★ spoon ★ flat plate

1. Brush the bowl with a little oil. Line it with cling film, getting rid of any bubbles.

2. Spoon a layer of ice-cream all round the bowl. Put it in the freezer while you mix the other ice-cream with the chocolate chips.

3. Fill the centre hole and smooth the surface. Put in the freezer for a few hours.

4. Let it stand to thaw for about 10 minutes. Place the plate on top and secure the cling film over it.

5. Turn it all upside down. Carefully lift the bowl clear. Someone may need to hold the plate for you!

6. Peel off the cling film. Press 12 chocolate fingers into the dome.

Smashing dome

Ask a grown-up to help in the kitchen.

Illustrations Stephanie Strickland

Ingredients
500g potatoes
★ knob of margarine
★ 6 sausages

You need
potato peeler ★ saucepan
★ knife ★ potato masher
★ spoon ★ plate

Peel or scrub the potatoes. Cut them into chunks then boil for about 10 minutes. Cut the sausages in half and grill them. Add the margarine to the potatoes and smash them to a mash. Pile it in a dome shape. Let the sausages cool a little then stick them in.

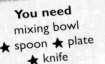

Dinky domes

You need
mixing bowl
★ spoon ★ plate
★ knife

QA Photos Ltd

Ingredients
150g icing sugar ★ 100g margarine
★ 1 tablespoon cream
★ 1 tablespoon cocoa powder
★ chocolate powder
★ hundreds and thousands
★ desiccated coconut

Mix the margarine, icing sugar and cream so it's fluffy. Add the cocoa powder and mix.
Shape into balls. Roll in the chocolate powder, hundreds and thousands or coconut. Leave in the fridge for an hour to cool.
Carefully cut in half.

Eat the dome before it melts!

Great Games

On 15th September the 27th Olympic Games will start in Sydney, Australia.

Sporting Pictures (UK) Ltd

First games

It started in Greece over two-and-a-half thousand years ago. It's thought the first Games were held in 776 BC. The word Olympic comes from Olympiad which describes the four years between the Games.

Sporting Pictures (UK) Ltd

Stop and start

The Games stopped in 394 AD. Just over a hundred years ago in 1896 (AD) the modern Games started – again in Greece.

First events

The first Olympics had one event called the stadium. It was a dash over a course about 185 metres long. In 708 BC the pentathlon was added. 'Pent' means five, so the pentathlon has five parts. These were running, wrestling, leaping, throwing the discus and hurling the spear. Athletes in the modern pentathlon do shooting, fencing, swimming, running and showjumping.

Oxford Scientific Films/Deni Bown

Olive crowns

At the first Olympics competitors won wreaths to wear on their heads. The wreaths were made from a special olive tree. An olive wreath pattern is on the medals that athletes win now.

XXVI OLYMPIAD ATLANTA 1996

Sporting Pictures (UK) Ltd

44

Getting bigger

In 1896, 311 competitors from 13 countries took part. The Sydney 2000 Games will have more than 10,000 athletes from 198 countries taking part in 28 sports. The Paralympics, for athletes with a disability, were first held in Rome in 1960. At the Sydney 2000 Paralympic Games, starting on 18th October, there will be 4,000 athletes from 125 countries competing in 18 sports.

Sporting Pictures (UK) Ltd

Flaming start

The Torch used to start the Olympics is lit from the sun's rays in Greece then carried by athletes to the Games. From 12th May the Torch will travel round Greece before a 17,000 kilometre journey through 12 island countries in the Pacific Ocean. On 8th June it starts a journey through all of Australia's states and territories to arrive in Sydney for the opening ceremony.

Sporting Pictures (UK) Ltd

Olympic signs

Each Olympic ring represents a continent. The flag of every country that takes part in the Games contains at least one of the five colours. The Olympic flag was first flown at the 1920 Games in Belgium.

Words to watch

★ **BC** (Before Christ) are dates more than two thousand years ago. ★ **AD** (Anno Domini which means 'in the year of our Lord') is used for dates now. ★ A **millennium** is one thousand years.

Mind-bogglers

Hop Till You Drop

Hop round the islands. Use the colourful letters to find the capital of Greece.

A puzzle that's all Greek.

Pick a beach to lie on, then admire the Aegean Sea.

Tuck into yummy goat's cheese.

Sample some houmous in Naxos.

This is the capital. What's it called?

☐ ☐ ☐ ☐ ☐ ☐

Sail to page 76 to see how well you did.

AEGEAN

CORFU

IONIAN SEA

NAXOS

SEA

RHODES

Start in the Ionian Islands.

It's said Theseus fought the Minotaur on Crete!

CRETE

Chomp through some juicy olives in Rhodes.

Illustrations Nick Diggory

45

Pet Rabbit

Rabbits can be fun pets! Make sure you really know how to look after rabbits before getting them.

Never alone

A rabbit is really unhappy living alone, so make sure it's got company. Two sisters living together is best as they will be used to one another. Rabbits that don't know each other can take time to get on. It's best they start living together when they are nine to twelve weeks old. You must make sure you play with your rabbit every day as well. To stop them fighting, breeding and getting some illnesses all rabbits should be neutered.

RSPCA/William S Paton

RSPCA/Damion Diplock

Room to move

Rabbits need loads of space. Make sure they have room to run and bounce about. The pen needs wire mesh walls so there's plenty of air but nothing can get in to hurt them. Put it somewhere they won't get wet, cold or hot.

A nice home

Inside the pen they need a hutch with two parts. The sleeping area should be about a quarter of the hutch with solid walls and piles of hay to make it cosy. The other end is for shelter in bad weather so also needs solid walls, but a wire mesh door on one side is a must for air and light. A rabbit-sized hole joins the two areas. The whole hutch must be raised off the ground with a ramp to the door.

RSPCA/E A Janes

Healthy food

Rabbits eat lots of green leafy things, root vegetables, fruit and hay. They need fresh supplies every day. They also need 'concentrates' twice a week. You buy these as pellets from the pet shop. Give rabbits clean water each day.

RSPCA/Andrew Linscott

RSPCA/Angela Hampton

Tessa's top tips

RSPCA/Tim Sambrook

Tessa Bailey, celebrity vet from TV's *Animal Hospital*, has these special rabbit-care tips.

- Rabbits need fresh green veg every day for healthy bones and teeth. A weekly treat of wholemeal bread, bananas or sweetcorn is OK.
- Play with your rabbit every day. Never chase after it though.
- Teach your rabbit to use a litter tray. It makes keeping it clean much easier.

Daily play

Don't be rough and never pick up a rabbit by its ears. Put your left hand on the back of its neck and your right hand under its bottom. Scoop the rabbit up and cradle it or hold it against you.

RSPCA/Angela Hampton

Looking good

A healthy rabbit is nice and round with shiny smooth fur. Its eyes should be clear and bright. Make sure its eyes and nose aren't runny. Check round its tail and its ears to make sure they are clean. If you think your rabbit isn't well make sure it is taken to a vet.

RSPCA/Angela Hampton

Two RSPCA rabbit booklets are available from Supplies Department, RSPCA, Causeway, Horsham, West Sussex RH12 1HG.

The RSPCA has an amazing kids club with an animal magazine and other goodies. Write to the RSPCA and mark your envelope 'Brownie Annual/Rabbits BA00'. The first 100 will get FREE membership. Don't forget to include your name, address and date of birth!

Thanks to the RSPCA for its help with this feature.

Cleaning

Rabbits must be kept clean. Each day replace any wet or dirty bedding and wash out the food dishes.

Take a look at the RSPCA web site at www.rspca.org.uk

The All-Purpose

The first verse contains a princess
Two witches (one evil, one good)
There is a castle in it somewhere
And a dark and tangled wood.

The second has ghosts and vampires
Monsters with foul-smelling breath
It sends shivers down the book spine
And scares everybody to death.

Illustration Kate Wells

48

Children's Poem

The third is one of my favourites
With rabbits in skirts and trousers
Who talk to each other like we do
And live in neat little houses.

The fourth verse is bang up to date
And in it anything goes.
Set in the city, it doesn't rhyme
(Although, in a way it does).

The fifth is set in the future
(And as you can see, it's the last)
When the Word was made Computer
And books are a thing of the past.

Roger McGough

Millennium

Get stuck into the last 2000 years of the world... and more! Time to boggle your brain...

Picture postcard!

Check out these old and not-so-old building wonders! Where on the time line would you put them?

A — Stonehenge

B — Empire State Building, New York

C — Hadrian's Wall

D — Great Wall of China

E — Taj Mahal, India

F — St Basil's Moscow

G — Millennium Dome

H — Leaning Tower of Pisa, Italy

I — Giza, Egypt

Trip/H Rogers

Trip/S Hill

Trip/D Morgan

Trip/H Rogers

Trip/B Turner

QA Photos Ltd

Trip/G Taylor

Trip/H Rogers

Time line

BC — 2550 — 2200 — 221 — 0 — 122 — 1350 — 1552 — 1629 — 1931 — 1999 — AD

World!

Too many 2000s

Put the 2000 shapes back together!
How many 2000s have you made?

Mosaic muddle!

How many 2000s can you
see in this ancient mosaic?

Know about the past? Ready for the future? Find out on page 76.

Illustrations Tom Clayton

Martian Munches

Fight off the black hole of hunger with these taste-bud ticklers straight from an alien menu!

 Ask a grown-up to help in the kitchen.

Star slime

Ingredients
undiluted blackcurrant squash ★ green jelly ★ orange juice ★ lemonade

You need
ice-cube trays ★ jug ★ glasses ★ straws

1. Fill one ice-cube tray with the blackcurrant squash. Put it in the freezer until it's solid.

2. Make the jelly using the packet instructions. Let it cool a little then pour it into the other ice-cube tray to set.

3. Put some jelly cubes in the bottom of each glass. Half fill with orange juice, top up with lemonade. Drop in a couple of blackcurrant cubes.

Slurp up the slime through a straw!

Cosmic crunch

Ingredients
75g margarine ★ I tablespoon golden syrup ★ 225g muesli ★ 25g chopped dates ★ 50g glacé cherries ★ 25g chocolate chips

You need
saucepan ★ wooden spoon ★ chopping board ★ knife ★ shallow baking tin ★ knife ★ cooking foil

1. Melt the margarine and golden syrup in the pan. Take it off the heat. Stir in the muesli, dates, cherries and choc chips until it's well mixed.

2. Press it into the tin and leave in the fridge for a few hours to set. Cut it into slices.

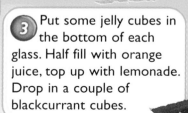

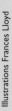

Juicy Jupiter

Ingredients
muffin ★ 25g grated cheese
★ 2 sliced mushrooms
★ I sliced tomato

You need
knife ★ chopping board

1 Halve the muffin. Toast it lightly. Cover with a layer of sliced tomatoes, then a layer of mushrooms. Keep two tomato slices spare.

2 Sprinkle with cheese. Place a slice of tomato on each half. Grill for 5 minutes. Leave to cool a little before eating.

Try making other planets!

BADGE WORK

I fancy making Neptune nibbles

Did you know

Space Snacks

Ever wondered what an astronaut eats deep in space? How different is it to meals on Earth?

TRH/NASA

Bags of energy
Being an astronaut is really hard work. They need lots of energy and must stay fit and healthy. The astronauts like their food to be tasty as well.

Small space
There's no kitchen in a space ship. Before they leave, the astronauts' food is carefully prepared. All they have to do is either heat it or add water.

Ready food
The astronauts need to decide before the mission what they are going to eat each day. They have a choice from over 70 hot and cold meals, as well as drinks. Each space meal is packed and looks like the meals you can buy in supermarkets.

Eat often
Astronauts eat three meals a day. The meal often comes on a tray that they strap to their legs so it doesn't float around. Knives, forks and plates are tied to the tray so they do not float away either!

TRH/NASA

53

Back To The Future

Do you know your jargon? Galaxies, solar system, universe, planets and stars. They are all out there.

A galaxy!

A galaxy is made up of millions of stars like our Sun. Our galaxy is called the Milky Way. It is vast and contains over 200 billion stars including all the stars we can see.

The solar system

The Earth is a planet and round it spins a moon. The Earth spins round the Sun. Another eight planets also spin round the Sun. Each one follows a different path called an orbit. All together this is called the solar system.

Blast from the past!

Scientists believe that Earth and all the other planets began millions of years ago with an enormous explosion called the Big Bang! The sun was formed 500 million years ago. The planets appeared 200 million years ago.

The Sun is our local star. It's a massive ball of burning gases fed from a central core. Without the Sun we wouldn't have heat and light.

On Mercury it can get very hot as it's so close to the Sun.

Web views
Check out these great addresses:
★ www.nasa.gov
★ sci.esa.int
★ www.stsci.edu

The air on Venus is poisonous and too hot for anything to live.

Two-thirds of the surface of our planet Earth is covered with water.

Mars has two moons. Its dusty surface has canyons and mountains.

Out of this world

★ It would take four months to travel to the Sun, but you'd melt before you got there!

★ Uranus is almost six years away from the Earth in a rocket.

★ It'll take more than 10 million years for footprints on the moon to disappear because there is no rain or wind.

Oxford Scientific Films/NASA

BADGE WORK   BROWNIE GUIDES

Sometimes Pluto is so far from the Sun its air freezes.

Living out in space

It only takes the space shuttle about eight and a half minutes to get into space! At the moment the space shuttle goes into space for about ten days. Astronauts can spend longer in space if they stay at a space station. A new international space station is being built at the moment. The first part is already in place.

Oxford Scientific Films/NASA

Neptune has lots of incredibly wild storms.

Uranus is very blue and four times bigger than Earth.

The ring round Saturn is made from chunks of ice.

The largest planet, Jupiter, has 16 moons, one is bigger than Pluto.

55

Wild Animal

This is your chance to win an amazingly animal prize. Enter this cool competition and you could be the lucky winner.

The prize

The winning Brownie and her friend get to meet Tessa Bailey at the RSPCA's TV *Animal Hospital* in London. There's a special tour to find out all about the animals being looked after and all the work that goes into making them better. Then it's on to Rainforest Cafe in London's West End for some tasty nosh. Finally is the fun of a sleepover in the Guide Heritage Centre. Review Travel will make sure you get to London and back, so you don't have to worry about that!

A WILD PLACE
TO SHOP AND EAT®

Rainforest Cafe

Read this!

The prize is for Tuesday 18th or Wednesday 19th April 2000. You've got to be sure you, your friend and an adult can make one of these dates.

Adventure

Competition

1. Create a cyber-pet for the future. Draw what it looks like and show at least five of these:
   - what it eats and drinks.
   - how and when it sleeps.
   - the sort of home it is happiest in.
   - how to keep it clean.
   - what sort of exercise it needs.
   - how to make it better when it's ill.
   - it's best and worst habits.

2. On the back of your entry write:
   - your name.
   - your age.
   - your address.
   - your favourite three things from this Annual.
   - the page where Tessa gives her top tips for keeping rabbits.

3. Seal your entry in an envelope and send it to:
   2000 Brownie Annual Pet Competition
   17–19 Buckingham Palace Road
   London SW1W 0PT
   Don't forget the stamp!

Hurry! The closing date is Monday 31st January 2000.

RSPCA/Ken McKay

RSPCA/Ken McKay

Heritage Centre

The Guide Association/Diana Aynaci

Olympic Feats

Here's your chance to go for gold. Pit yourself against the trials of the Brownie Sixathlon.

Hosting the games

The games can be held in a garden, playground or park. On grass is best, just make sure there's nothing sharp about. Make sure your ref knows all the rules.

Let a grown-up know where you are going.

- ✱ Make a special banner for your opening ceremony.
- ✱ Team colours and a mascot keep your Six spirits high!
- ✱ Medals are a must. Bake or make before the event.
- ✱ Each Six needs its winner's tune for the medal ceremony.

You need

a Brownie Six ✱ your sports kit ✱ a grown-up, or older brother or sister as ref ✱ a watch with a second hand ✱ some water – it's thirsty work ✱ food cans or drinks bottles to use as markers ✱ baton made from short card tube ✱ a hoop ✱ bean bag or tennis ball ✱ tape measure

Relay

Measure a certain distance with two markers. Half the Six stands at one marker, the other half at the other. The first runner sprints the distance with the baton. She hands it to the second runner who runs back. Keep going until everyone has run the distance.

Edible Medal

Get stuck in

The perfect reward for an Olympic challenge!

Ask a grown-up to pre-heat the oven to 180°C or gas mark 4.

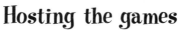

1. Mix the sugar and margarine. Add the egg, flour and mixed spice.

2. Mix into a dough. Roll the dough so it's at least 1cm thick.

3. Press out biscuits with the large cutter. Make a hole in the middle and a small hole at the top.

4. Line the tray and bake for five minutes. Add boiled sweet to each one. Bake for another five minutes. When they are cool add a ribbon.

Ingredients

120g soft brown sugar ★ 120g margarine ★ a small egg, beaten ★ 250g plain flour ★ 2 teaspoon mixed spice ★ 30 round boiled sweets

You need

mixing bowl ★ sieve ★ spoon ★ mug ★ fork ★ rolling pin ★ large and small round biscuit cutters ★ straw ★ greaseproof paper ★ baking tray ★ ribbon

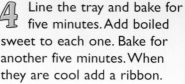

Illustrations Stephanie Strickland

58

Target hitting

Place two markers ten big steps apart. Stand at one and throw three hoops at the other.

Gymnastics

Each do three forward rolls one after another. Then three cartwheels one after another. The ref decides who's best.

Long throw

Stand by a marker. Throw a bean bag from your shoulder as far as you can.

Kayak slalom

Set up markers like this. Half the Six stands at one end and the rest at the other end. Weave in and out following the route. Hand the baton from player to player until everyone's had a go.

Jump

Stand by a marker. Jump as far as possible, keeping your feet together.

Training

Get together with your friends or Six. Practice hard! Make sure you can hand over the relay baton quickly without dropping it. Who's best at going first and last? Check out who can balance for the gymnastics. Who's got the knack at throwing hoops? Got your team worked out? Challenge another Six to an Olympic competition.

Brownie photographs Diana Aynaci

I'm Bored!

Louise loves everything about animals and the environment.

Wow! My birthday present?

This'll help me get my bird watcher badge…

…and I can do the RSPB's Big Garden Bird Watch survey!

At Brownies Kate got a special badge.

Your Friend To Animals badge!

Well done, Kate!

I'm really pleased. I never thought I'd get this.

Yeah, but gerbils are great pets!

I know! Burger and Fries are really cute!

And you help at the vet's! You're so jammy!

Ready? Sam's waiting for us.

Yeah, okay! Let's go!

Louise and Kate dawdle behind Sam.

Looks like Sarah's been playing football.

Been to Brownies?

Yeah.

Give me football any day!

We had a real laugh!

Yeah? What did you do, then?

Kate got a badge.

What for?

It's for being good to animals.

Sounds boring to me, you wouldn't catch me there.

Brownies isn't as boring as football!

On Saturday...

It's great watching the birds.

Cool present! What else do they eat?

Wish I had a garden. Then I could feed the birds, too.

Hey, I've got just the thing. Wait here!

Bird seed, nuts, dried porridge oats. They need loads of water, too.

This is my old one, but it still works.

Great! Thanks!

See these suckers? They'll stick to your window!

What's next? Turn over to find out.

Photographs by Diana Aynaci

63

Planet-saver

How much do you really know about saving the planet for the next millennium?

Bin it!
Put things in the right place for recycling.

Lost leaves
Match the leaves with the fruit.

Growing

You need
★ tree sapling
★ shovel or spade
★ bucket of water
★ rabbit guard (if necessary)
★ tape measure

Ask a grown-up for help.

Cut out and colour in
your special Brownie
Annual bookmark

Bookmark

Brownie annual 2000

Brownie magazine

Have you ever seen *BROWNIE* magazine? It's full of puzzles, stories, recipes, things to make, fascinating facts, and news about other Brownies.

If you would like to receive your own copy of the magazine every month, please fill in your details here.

Please send me a subscription form for *BROWNIE* magazine.

Name ....

Pack ....

Address ....

....

.... Postcode ....

2

Publications (BA 2000)
FREEPOST (LON 145)
The Guide Association
LONDON
SW1W 0YA

New uses

Spot the ten things Suzi's made from items that were going to be thrown out.

Getting greener? Turn to page 76 for the answer.

Now try this

Planet

Planting a tree helps the planet grow for the new millennium!

Nice spot!

Trees like plenty of light. Their roots need room to grow, so don't plant it close to a building or a path.

1 Dig a hole 30cm across and 30cm deep. Dip the roots in water. Pop the tree in the hole. Is there enough room for the roots to grow? If not, make the hole bigger.

2 Fill the hole a little at a time, pressing the earth gently as you go until the roots are all covered. Gently press down with your feet.

3 Check the tree is firmly in place. Wrap round some rabbit guard. Water the tree well and watch it grow!

Illustrations Stephanie Strickland

Table Top

Stage your own Euro 2000 with this exciting football game!

You need

newspaper or plastic sheet ★ a piece of card or board about 120cm x 70cm ★ pencil and ruler ★ green paint ★ broad paintbrush ★ white paint ★ thin paintbrush ★ black oil-based model paint ★ cocktail stick ★ plasticine ★ thin garden cane (at least 85cm) ★ hacksaw ★ 12 kitchen twists ★ netting, eg from a fruit bag ★ two straws ★ ping-pong ball

1 Cover the area you're going to work on with newspaper. Paint the card green. Let it dry.

2 Lightly mark in pencil all the lines shown. Carefully paint them white. Let them dry.

‹ 10·5 ›
‹5·5›
50CM ‹ 9 CM ›
5
7·5
10·5
9CM
1CM
50 CM

3 Paint the ping-pong ball to look like a football. A cocktail stick attached to the ball with a blob of plasticine makes it easier! Let it dry.

66

Team

④ Cut the cane into four 11cm lengths and two 20cm lengths. Use the kitchen ties to attach two short uprights to the crossbar.

Get a grown-up to show you how to use a hacksaw safely.

⑤ Attach a goal to each end with a lump of plasticine. Hang netting over the back. Secure with kitchen twists. Bend all ends out of the way.

⑥ Practise on your pitch with the ball and straw. Find an opponent and test your skills.

Follow the action

There's masses of useful info and the latest hot football news on these top web sites.

www.fifa.com
www.scottishfa.co.uk
www.fa-premier.com
www.on-the-ball.com

Check them out!

Remember to wash all the brushes before they dry!

Illustrations Frances Lloyd

67

Know The Score

Euro 2000 will make it an exciting summer. Be ready to kick off with these fantastic footie facts!

The team

Football is played by two teams of 11 players. Each team has substitutes who are swapped if a player is injured or not playing well.

Player positions

The goalkeeper protects the goal and usually organises the defence. The main job of defenders is to stop the other team scoring. Midfielders defend and attack, and get the ball to the strikers It's mainly down to the strikers to score the goals.

Jargon

Sub is another word for substitute player. The goalkeeper is sometimes called the goalie or the keeper. The referee can be called the ref. The opposition is the other team.

Kick off

The match starts with a kick off from the centre circle. A coin is flipped to decide which team kicks off.

Sporting Pictures UK Ltd

Sporting Pictures UK Ltd

goal

goal line

corner circle

goal area

halfway line

touchline

centre circle

penalty spot

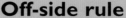

Out of play and goals

The ball is out of play when it's completely over the touchline or goal line. To start play again the ball is thrown-in from the side or kicked in from the corner. To score a goal, the ball must go completely over the goal line.

Off-side rule

A player in the opposition's half of the pitch is off-side when there aren't at least two opponents between her and the goal line. If the ref thinks this gives her team an unfair advantage the opposition gets a free kick.

Free kicks

If a player breaks the rules the ref can award a free kick to a player in the other team.

Action Images

Long shot

Over 2,000 years ago the Chinese played a game like soccer. The Romans also had a version, too!

Now try this

Skills

Close ball control is essential so master dribbling and passing.

Passing

Put your non-kicking foot near the ball. Turn your kicking leg from your hip.

The inside of your foot should be facing the way the ball will go.

Dribbling

First use the inside of your foot.

Straighten it up using the outside of your foot.

Then use the inside again. Keep going and build up a rhythm.

Follow through with your foot towards your target.

Illustrations Nick Diggory

69

The Ultimate

Goodbye old millennium, hello new one! It's going to be the ultimate party. Here's how to party all through the year.

Pick a theme

What's the party for? Is it your mate's birthday? Or is there some other great reason? Don't worry if there's no special occasion. Dream up your own ideas to make it the party of the year. Have a go at one of these:

★ **Tropical Hawaiian.**
★ **Space-age Stomp.**
★ **Fairytale Fantasy.**

Ready to party?

You'll need to make sure all your friends know that you're having a party. Design cool invites and send them out. Take a look at these.

> *Tiffany would love it if Joanne could be at her 9th Birthday party. It's at her house at 4 o'clock on Saturday 15 January 2000*

> Jane, Maxine, Emma, Chelsea and Frankie (the Leprechauns) are having a space-age party and want *Cheryl* to be there at 6pm on Friday 21 July. It's going to be at the Brownie hall and there'll be masses to eat. Remember to wear space-age gear or you don't get in!

> Sharini's party is going to happen at noon on Sunday 2 April at Wiltshire Road. There will be lots to eat, plenty of games and a present for everyone. Hope you can be there!

Make sure you say the day, the time and where it'll be. Ask them to let you know if they are coming.

Dazzling decs

Make lots of decorations to cheer the place up. Paint pictures onto thin card and stick them to the walls with something that won't leave a mark. Balloons and streamers are great, too. Look at these ideas.

Check with a grown-up that it's OK to have a party. Ask them to help with the food and decorations.

party

BADGE WORK · BROWNIE GUIDES

Fab food
Serve great grub with deliciously cool drinks.

Game on!
Have a few games to get everyone going.
Why not try these…
★ **Hawaiian dancer** Who dances the longest and the best to the tropical tunes?
★ **Just a human** Who can eat a sugary doughnut without licking her lips?
★ **Royal jewels** Everyone looks at ten bits of jewellery. Everyone closes their eyes and one thing is taken away. Who can work out what it was?
★ **Back bender** Who can limbo under the pole?

The coolest gear
Pick your favourite party clothes to wear. Make sure you look your best. If it's fancy dress really go for it! Don't be a party-pooper!

Don't forget to say thank you after going to a party.

Music
Bop till you drop to your fave bands. Pick the best groups to make sure everyone has a great time dancing. Sing along to your top tunes.

Illustrations Bill Ledger

Party Pick And Mix

Find out how much of a party animal you really are with these great brain benders!

Trendy togs!

Raid your wardrobe for a party to remember!
What items would you wear for these parties?

1 Summer sizzle ☐ ☐ ☐ ☐

2 Mellow yellow ☐ ☐ ☐

3 Winter wonder ☐ ☐ ☐ ☐

4 Combat capers ☐ ☐ ☐ ☐

5 Getting the blues ☐ ☐ ☐ ☐

Thirst quencher

Can you guess which crazy cocktail is which?

| Tutti Fruiti | Peach Punch Delight | Ice-cream Smoothie | Palm Tree Paradise | Pink Dreamer | Pineapple Star Surprise |

A B C D E F

Dazzling deccies!
Party time! Follow the balloon streamers to find out which one's movin' and shakin' to the end!

Party on to page 76 to find out how well you did.

Wrap it up!
Guess what's inside each party pressie!

73

Tempting

Fancy a new look? Want to win some great gear from NEXT's new range? Here's your chance.

NEXT

The prizes

Five lucky Brownies will each win a fab NEXT voucher worth £80. The winners can spend their prizes in any NEXT store nationwide. Choose from fleeces, combats, hooded tops, bootleg jeans and loads more! There are even hats, rucksacks, chunky trainers and groovy shoes.

What to do

1 Let us know your dream clothes for the new millennium. Design a range of items and outfits that you'd like to wear in the future. Make sure you include at least three things from this list:

❀ sizzling summer camping kit.
❀ super sporty games gear.
❀ fun party wear.
❀ amazing accessories.
❀ fabulous footwear.

Remember to use a combination of different fabrics and colours. The funky NEXT clothes in these photos might give you some ideas.

Trendy Togs

BADGE WORK

Look! You can even kit out your room!

2 On the back of your creation write:
- your name.
- your age.
- your address.
- your favourite three things from this Annual.
- the best thing you've ever done as a Brownie.

3 Pop your entry in an envelope and send it to:

2000 Brownie Annual/ Next Competition The Guide Association 17–19 Buckingham Palace Road London SW1W 0PT

Don't forget the stamp!

Better hurry! The closing date is Monday 31st January 2000.

Answers

Is Anyone Out There?
(front end paper)

The computer password is SOLAR SYSTEM.

Chinese Challenger!
(pages 8–9)

Message finder
The message in the square is:
Brownies is the best thing I do and I am going to have monster fun with my Annual.
Read from the top right-hand corner of the box down to the bottom left.

Light riddles
I am a DRAGON.

Enter the dragon (below)

Against The Clock
(page 13)

Hidden message is: Clocking up a winning time.

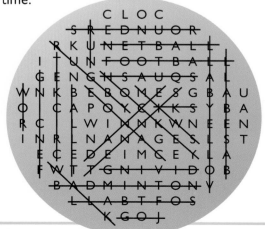

On The Ball!
(pages 16–17)

Hot shots
The player in the centre scored the goal (see above).

Football crazy
The fourth player is from another team (see below).

National players
England: fish and chips, double-decker bus and Stonehenge (4, 5 and 12) • *France:* cheese, Eiffel Tower and onions (3, 6 and 10) • *Italy:* opera singer, Venice gondola and pasta (2, 14 and 15) • *Netherlands:* tulip, windmill and clogs (7, 9 and 11) • *Scotland:* bagpipes, thistle and kilt (1, 8 and 13)

Fit For The Olympics!
(pages 28–29)

Olympic trivia
1c Sydney • 2c 28 • 3b Every 4 years • 4a With a torch • 5a Five rings • 6a Athletes with a disability

Sports gear (see right)

What a ball!
There are nine different types of balls being used. Table tennis, basketball, volleyball, softball, hockey, water polo, rugby, cricket and football.

Ride on (below)

Planet-saver
(pages 64–65)

Bin it! (right)

Lost leaves
- 1B holly
- 2E sycamore
- 3D horse chestnut
- 4A coconut
- 5C oak.

New uses
cork tiles (message board), kitchen roll (pencil holder), cereal packets (envelope holder), boxes under bed, old clothes on bed, shoe boxes over bed, coat hangers (chimes), biscuit tin (jewellery case), card (picture frame), jam jar (flower pot).

Hop Till You Drop
(page 45)

Athens is the capital of Greece.

Party Pick And Mix!
(pages 72–73)

Trendy togs
1 Summer sizzle AFRS • 2 Mellow yellow BKN • 3 Winter wonder CELP • 4 Combat capers DGIM • 5 Getting the blues HJOQ

Thirst quencher (see below)

Dazzling deccies!
Streamer A is attached to a balloon.

Wrap it up!
Jewellery • a radio-cassette player • make-up • a watch • pair of socks • a camera • a soft toy • a mobile phone.

Pink Dreamer · Pineapple Star Surprise · Palm Tree Paradise · Peach Punch Delight · Tutti Fruiti · Ice-cream Smoothie

A Star Turn
(pages 40–41)

Stargazing (below left)
Freda is the odd one out. Leo and the Bear are constellations.

Space to base
The three messages are:
- Earth is a very special planet!
- Can I be a Brownie?
- I'd like to be your friend.

Alien invasion (below)

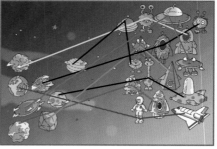

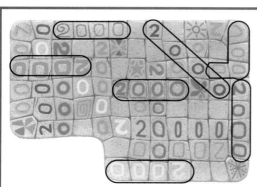

Millennium World! (pages 50–51)

Too many 2000s: There are six 2000s.

Mosaic muddle: There are seven complete 2000s in the mosaic (see left).

Picture postcard!

BC — I 2550 · 2200 · A D 221 · 0 · C 122 · 1350 · H F 1552 · 1629 · E B 1931 · G 1999 AD

Round The

Follow the Olympic torch as it travels to the 2000 Games in Australia!

You need
a dice ★
a counter each

Here's how
1 Shake six to start.
2 Follow any instructions you land on.
3 The player to reach Sydney first wins.

13

14 Fall off at water. Miss a go.

15

16 Swim one length too few. Go to 12.

17

18 Win at the high jump. Leap to 21.

19

20 Score the winning goal! Move on 3.

21

22 High dive! Move on 5.

23

24 Stop for a drink. Go to 26.

25

26

41 Trip up competitor. Go back to start.

False start. Go to 39.

40

42

43 Hit ball out of court. Miss a go.

44

45

46

47 Forget to put on your helmet. Go to 40.

48 Torch goes out. Miss a go.

49

SYDNEY

Illustration David Pattison